LAUGH
-Out-
LOUD
Valentine's Day
JOKES
for **KIDS**

LAUGH -Out- LOUD

Valentine's Day

JOKES for KIDS

ROB ELLIOTT

HARPER
An Imprint of HarperCollins Publishers

Library of Congress Control Number: 2020942250
ISBN 978-0-06-299186-7

21 22   PC/BRR   10 9 8 7 6 5 4 3
❖
First Edition

Valentine's Day is about celebrating the ones we love and those who love us. This book is first dedicated to my forever valentine, Joanna. I also dedicate this book to my six amazing kids and wonderful family and friends. If there was ever a time in life to laugh and celebrate each day with the people we love, it's now.

Q: What did one marshmallow say to the other?

A: "I want s'more time with you!"

Q: Why did the bee marry the rabbit?

A: She was his honey bunny.

Knock, knock.

Who's there?

Parmesan.

Parmesan who?

Do I have Parmesan to take you to the Valentine's dance?

Q: **Why did the boy and girl play tennis on their date?**

A: It was a court-ship.

Q: **What did the farmer give his wife for Valentine's Day?**

A: A hog and kiss!

Q: **How did the farmer show his wife he loved her?**

A: He brought home the bacon.

Q: **Who did the monster go out with on Valentine's Day?**

A: His ghoul-friend.

Knock, knock.

Who's there?

Joanna.

Joanna who?

Joanna be my valentine?

Q: How do gardeners kiss?

A: With their tulips.

Q: What did A send B on Valentine's Day?

A: A love letter.

Q: What did the dolphin do when his girlfriend broke up with him?

A: He whaled!

- -

Q: What do cows like to do on Valentine's Day?

A: Cud-dle.

Knock, knock.

Who's there?

Raisin.

Raisin who?

You're the raisin I'm so happy!

Knock, knock.

Who's there?

Owl.

Owl who?

Owl always love you!

Knock, knock.

Who's there?

Wooden shoe.

Wooden shoe who?

Wooden shoe like to be my valentine?

Knock, knock.

Who's there?

Fondue.

Fondue who?

I'm very fondue you!

Knock, knock.

Who's there?

Frank.

Frank who?

Frank you for loving me.

Q: What happened when the cow didn't get any valentines?

A: She felt moooo-dy!

Q: What did the girl snake say to the boy snake?

A: "Will you be my boa-friend?"

- -

Q: Why did the cows get married?

A: They were udder-ly in love!

Q: What did the wasp say to the bum-blebee on Valentine's Day?

A: "You're my bee-loved."

Q: Why don't polar bears and pen-guins fall in love?

A: Because they're polar opposites.

Q: What did the skunk say when his girlfriend broke up with him?

A: "Love stinks!"

Knock, knock.

Who's there?

Abby.

Abby who?

Abby Valentine's Day!

Q: What happened when the vampire met his blind date?

A: It was love at first bite.

Q: How do you throw a Valentine's Day party on the moon?

A: You planet.

Knock, knock.

Who's there?

Wool.

Wool who?

Wool you be my valentine?

Q: What do you serve a boxer at a Valentine's Day party?

A: Punch and cookies.

Q: Why shouldn't you date a sausage?

A: Because they're the wurst!

Q: Why did the turtle have a bad time with her date?

A: He wouldn't come out of his shell.

Q: Why did the horse break up with her boyfriend?

A: He didn't seem stable.

Q: Why did the tree get back together with his girlfriend?

A: They were turning over a new leaf.

Q: **What did the snakes do after their fight?**

A: They hissed and made up.

Q: **Why did the lion break up with his girlfriend?**

A: Because she was a cheetah.

Q: **How does a bison pay for dinner and a movie?**

A: It uses buffalo bills.

Q: **What did the wasp say to his girlfriend?**

A: "Will you bee my valentine?"

Q: Where did the computer pro-grammer take his girlfriend on Valentine's Day?

A: For a byte to eat.

Q: Why did the sheep break up with her boyfriend?

A: Because he was baaaaaa-d.

Q: What did the sheep say to his girl-friend?

A: "I love ewe!"

Q: What do you call it when two boats fall in love?

A: A relation-ship.

Q: **What do you give a knitter for Valentine's Day?**

A: Diamonds and purls.

Knock, knock.

Who's there?

Donate.

Donate who?

Donate make sense for you to be my valentine?

Q: **Where do tarantulas look for love?**

A: On dating web-sites.

Q: What do you give your dad on Valentine's Day?

A: Lolli-pops.

Q: What do bad guys give on February 14th?

A: Villain-tines.

Q: What did the stamp say to the envelope?

A: "I'm stuck on you."

Q: Why do skunks celebrate Valentine's Day?

A: They're very scent-imental.

Q: What's the best thing to do on February 14th?

A: Party heart-y!

Q: Why did the horse stay home on Valentine's Day?

A: It decided to hit the hay!

Q: How did the golfers celebrate Valentine's Day?

A: They had a tee party.

Q: **What did the bat say to his girlfriend?**

A: "I like hanging out with you."

Q: **Why do maple trees love Valentine's Day?**

A: They're very sappy.

Q: **Why did the noses break up?**

A: They kept picking on each other.

Q: **What did the chef give his wife for Valentine's Day?**

A: A hug and a quiche.

Jim: Joe, do you have a date for Valentine's Day?

Joe: I sure do—it's February 14th!

Q: Why can't sunglasses get a date on Valentine's Day?

A: They're shady!

Q: Why did the meteorologist cancel her date?

A: She was feeling under the weather.

Q: How did the broom know it was in love?

A: It was swept off its feet.

Knock, knock.

Who's there?

Russian.

Russian who?

I'm Russian to finish making my valentines!

Q: What happened to the atoms when they got in fight?

A: They split up!

Q: **What kind of shoes do you wear to surprise your valentine?**

A: Sneakers.

Q: **Why did the dragons plan a date for Valentine's Day?**

A: They wanted a knight on the town.

Q: **Why wouldn't the door go out with the window on Valentine's Day?**

A: It was a pane!

Q: **When does a duck wake up on Valentine's Day?**

A: At the quack of dawn.

Q: **Why did the librarian turn down her date for Valentine's Day?**

A: She was already booked.

Q: **What happens if you forget to give a frog a valentine?**

A: It will feel unhoppy.

Knock, knock.

Who's there?

Weirdo.

Weirdo who?

Weirdo we go to celebrate Valentine's Day?

Q: Why did the tailor and the quilter get married?

A: Because they were sew in love!

Q: Why did the calendar feel stressed on Valentine's Day?

A: It had too many dates to choose from.

Knock, knock.

Who's there?

Police.

Police who?

Police be my valentine!

Q: Why do baseball players always take their dates to restaurants?

A: They like to stay behind the plate.

Q: What begins with a P, ends with an E, and has millions of letters?

A: A post office on Valentine's Day.

Knock, knock.

Who's there?

Annie.

Annie who?

Annie valentines for me today?

Q: What did the horse say when its date didn't show up for dinner?

A: "That's the last straw!"

Q: What do you get when a butcher and a baker get married?

A: Meat loaf.

Knock, knock.

Who's there?

Juicy.

Juicy who?

Juicy any reason why you shouldn't be my valentine?

Q: Why did the fig stay home on Valentine's Day?

A: It couldn't get a date.

Q: What do you call two birds in love?

A: Tweet-hearts.

Q: What did one leaf say to the other leaf?

A: "I think I'm falling for you."

Pony: How was your Valentine's Day?

Horse: Not good!

Pony: What happened?

Horse: My date was a night-mare!

Q: **Why did the bird stay home from the Valentine's dance?**

A: It was too chicken to go!

Knock, knock.

Who's there?

Pudding.

Pudding who?

I'm pudding the final touches on my valentines.

Q: How does an oyster get in touch with its girlfriend?

A: It texts her on its shell phone.

Knock, knock.

Who's there?

Willie.

Willie who?

Willie ask her to be his valentine?

Knock, knock.

Who's there?

Yoda.

Yoda who?

Yoda one for me!

Knock, knock.

Who's there?

Pooch.

Pooch who?

Pooch your arms around me.

Q: Why did the baker buy diamonds for his girlfriend?

A: He had a lot of dough.

Q: Why did the pony have to cancel its date for Valentine's Day?

A: It was a little horse.

Q: What do you give a pig on February 14th?

A: A valen-swine.

Q: Where did the polar bear take its date for Valentine's Day?

A: To the snow ball.

Q: Why did the gymnast change her plans on Valentine's Day?

A: She was flexible.

Q: **What happened to the clam at the Valentine's Day dance?**

A: It pulled a mussel.

Q: **What did the baker say on her wedding day?**

A: "I loaf you with all my heart!"

Q: **What happened when the strawberry scheduled two dates on Valentine's Day?**

A: It was in a jam!

Q: **What did one magnet say to the other magnet?**

A: "I'm very attracted to you!"

Q: How did the fisherman meet new people?

A: He net-worked.

Q: Why did the bananas cancel their date for Valentine's Day?

A: They split up!

Q: What did the cheese say to his bride?

A: "I want to grow mold together."

Q: What did the boa constrictor say to the mouse?

A: "I think I have a crush on you!"

Q: What did the apple say to the banana?

A: "I think you're ap-peeling!"

Knock, knock.

Who's there?

Noah.

Noah who?

Noah good place to take a date for Valentine's Day?

Knock, knock.

Who's there?

Howard.

Howard who?

Howard you like to be my valentine?

Q: Why did the collie break up with the German shepherd?

A: It wanted to paws from dating for a while.

Q: Why did the slug break up with the snail?

A: The relationship was moving too slow.

Q: Why did the candies fall in love?

A: They were mint for each other.

Q: What did the boy cat say to the girl cat?

A: "We're purr-fect for each other!"

Q: What did the ice cream say to the Popsicle?

A: "You melt my heart."

Q: Why did the mittens get married?

A: It was glove at first sight.

Knock, knock.

Who's there?

Muffin.

Muffin who?

I've muffin to offer you but love!

Q: Why did the scientists fall in love?

A: They had great chemistry.

Q: Why did the algebra teacher break up with the geometry teacher?

A: Something just didn't add up!

Knock, knock.

Who's there?

Atlas.

Atlas who?

Atlas it's Valentine's Day!

Q: Why won't a lobster buy you a valentine?

A: They're penny-pinchers.

Q: Why did the couple eat fruit for breakfast every morning?

A: They wanted to live apple-y ever after.

Q: Did you hear about the bedbugs that fell in love?

A: They are getting married in the spring!

Knock, knock.

Who's there?

Hollywood.

Hollywood who?

Hollywood you like to be my valentine?

Knock, knock.

Who's there?

Ada.

Ada who?

Ada lot of Valentine's candy, so now I feel sick.

Q: What did the baker say to his wife on Valentine's Day?

A: "I knead you!"

Q: Why doesn't the tin man like Valentine's Day?

A: He's heartless.

Q: What kind of song do you play on February 14th?

A: A valen-tune.

Q: What happened when the teddy bear ate all the Valentine's chocolates?

A: It was stuffed.

Knock, knock.

Who's there?

Iguana.

Iguana who?

Iguana be your valentine.

Knock, knock.

Who's there?

Toad.

Toad who?

Have I toad you lately that I love you?

Knock, knock.

Who's there?

Otter.

Otter who?

You otter be my valentine.

Q: Where did the pigs go on their honeymoon?

A: New Ham-pshire.

Q: **Why did the pig have such a bad time with her Valentine's date?**

A: He was such a boar!

Knock, knock.

Who's there?

Melon.

Melon who?

You're one in a melon!

Q: **Why did the astronauts break up?**

A: They needed some space.

Knock, knock.

Who's there?

Casino.

Casino who?

Casino reason why you shouldn't be my valentine.

Q: Why did the rabbit stay home from the Valentine's dance?

A: It was having a bad hare day!

Knock, knock.

Who's there?

Jimmy.

Jimmy who?

Jimmy a little kiss on the cheek.

Q: Why did the girl break up with the baker?

A: Because he was a weir-dough!

Q: How can you make your dog laugh on Valentine's Day?

A: Give it a funny bone!

Q: What did the werewolf say to his girlfriend?

A: "Fang you for being my valentine."

Knock, knock.

Who's there?

Irish.

Irish who?

Irish you would be my valentine!

Knock, knock.

Who's there?

Anita.

Anita who?

Anita get some candy and flowers for my valentine!

Jenny: How was your date with the baseball player?

Jan: He knocked it out of the park!

Q: Why don't you want to date a meteorologist?

A: They always have their head in the clouds.

Q: What month is it hard to tell the truth?

A: Fib-ruary.

Q: Why do oysters make bad dates?

A: They always clam up on you.

Knock, knock.

Who's there?

Anna.

Anna who?

Anna chance you'll be my valentine?

Q: What happened when the sea lions fell in love?

A: They sealed it with a kiss.

Q: What did Robin Hood say to his girlfriend?

A: "I Sherwood love to be your valentine."

**Q: What did the baker wear on his
  date?**

A: His new loaf-ers!

**Q: Why did the monsters go out on
  Valentine's Day?**

A: They found each other eerie-sistible!

Knock, knock.

Who's there?

Window.

Window who?

**Window we get to open our valen-
  tines?**

Q: What did the biker say to his girl-friend?

A: "I wheelie like you."

Q: Why did the frogs get married?

A: They were toad-ally in love!

Q: What did the snake give her boy-friend for Valentine's Day?

A: A little hissss on the cheek.

Q: What did the whale say to his girl-friend on Valentine's Day?

A: "You're fin-tastic!"

Knock, knock.

Who's there?

Bacon.

Bacon who?

I'm bacon you a cake for Valentine's Day!

Q: What do pilgrims give each other on Valentine's Day?

A: Mayflowers.

Q: Why are painters so romantic?

A: They'll love you with all their art.

Q: **What did the volcano say to the mountain?**

A: "I'd lava to be your valentine!"

Q: **What did the computer do after it got home late from the Valentine's party?**

A: It crashed.

Q: **What do you say if a porcupine gives you a kiss?**

A: "Ouch!"

Q: **Why shouldn't you date a mathematician?**

A: They have too many problems!

Knock, knock.

Who's there?

Donuts.

Donuts who?

I'm donuts about you!

**Q: Why did the girl go to the doctor
on Valentine's Day?**

A: She was lovesick!

**Q: Why did the girl have a crush on
the fisherman?**

A: He was quite a catch.

Q: Why did the squirrels go on a date?

A: They were nuts about each other!

Knock, knock.

Who's there?

Luke.

Luke who?

Luke who got a valentine!

Q: What did the caveman give his wife on Valentine's Day?

A: Ughs and kisses.

Q: Why did the couple go bungee jumping on Valentine's Day?

A: They were falling for each other.

Q: **What do you get when you cross Bigfoot and Shakespeare?**

A: Romeo and Juli-yeti.

Q: **Why did the sharks get engaged?**

A They wanted to make it o-fish-al.

Q: **Why did the boy break up with the tennis player?**

A: She made too much racket.

Q: **Why can't you surprise a mountain for Valentine's Day?**

A: They're always peak-ing.

Knock, knock.

Who's there?

Mustache.

Mustache who?

I mustache you to be my valentine.

Leah: How was your date with the author?

Anna: It was all write.

Anna: I got a huge box of chocolates for Valentine's Day!

Leah: Sweet!

Q: What did the groundhog say to his girlfriend?

A: "I dig you."

Q: Why did the panther break up with the tiger?

A: She was always lion.

Knock, knock.

Who's there?

Orange.

Orange who?

Orange you glad you're my valentine?

Knock, knock.

Who's there?

Emma.

Emma who?

Emma hoping I get a lot of valentines this year!

Q: What did the possum say to his girlfriend?

A: "Will you hang out with me?"

Knock, knock.

Who's there?

Dishes.

Dishes who?

Dishes going to be the best Valentine's Day yet!

Q: Why don't you want to date a chicken?

A: They're cheep!

Q: Did you hear about the blender that married the spoon?

A: It caused quite a stir.

Knock, knock.

Who's there?

Riley.

Riley who?

I Riley want to be your valentine!

Q: What kind of bug loves Valentine's Day?

A: A hopeless roman-tick.

Q: When do you give astronauts their wedding presents?

A: At their meteor shower!

Q: **Why did the farmer ask the florist to go on a date?**

A: It was a budding romance.

Q: **What did the worm say to her blind date?**

A: "Where on earth have you been all my life?"

Q: **Why did the girl turn down a date with the sailor?**

A: There was something fishy about him.

Q: Why is it a bad idea to date a firefly?

A: They need to lighten up!

Q: Why does a mushroom have a date every weekend?

A: He's a fungi!

Q: What do you get when you cross a dog and a dozen roses?

A: Collie-flower!

Knock, knock.

Who's there?

Ethan.

Ethan who?

Ethan if you forget my valentine, I still like you!

Q: Where did the cats go on their date?

A: Out for mice cream.

Knock, knock.

Who's there?

Alibi.

Alibi who?

Alibi the chocolate if you get the flowers.

Knock, knock.

Who's there?

Honeydew.

Honeydew who?

Honeydew you think you can be my valentine?

Knock, knock.

Who's there?

Heidi.

Heidi who?

Heidi Valentine's chocolates before I
eat them all!

Knock, knock.

Who's there?

Butcher.

Butcher who?

Butcher arms around me and give me
a hug.

Natalee: Did you enjoy your date with the surgeon?

Cheri: Yes, he had me in stitches the whole time.

Q: What happened after the pig's girlfriend moved away?

A: They became pen pals.

Knock, knock.

Who's there?

Megan.

Megan who?

Megan my valentines for all my friends.

Q: Why did the potato break up with the radish?

A: He was a dead-beet.

Q: Why did the cyclops break up with her boyfriend?

A: He'd never look her in the eye.

Q: What did the lipstick say to the eye shadow after their fight?

A: "Let's kiss and makeup."

Knock, knock.

Who's there?

Oscar.

Oscar who?

Oscar if she'll be your valentine.

Q: What do you get when you cross a bike and a bouquet of roses?

A: Flower pedals.

Q: What happened when the kangaroos got married?

A: They lived hop-pily ever after.

Q: Why did the girl break up with the trumpet player?

A: He was always tooting his own horn.

Q: Why did all the girls have a crush on the guitar player?

A: He pulled on their heart strings.

Q: What did the lumberjack ask his girlfriend on Valentine's Day?

A: "Wood you be mine?"

Q: What kind of candy do you give a scientist for Valentine's Day?

A: Experi-mints!

Q: **Where did the rabbits go after their wedding?**

A: On their bunny-moon.

Knock, knock.

Who's there?

Mushroom.

Mushroom who?

Not mushroom to write on this valentine!

Q: **Why did the porcupine get sent home from the Valentine's party?**

A: It was popping all the balloons.

Q: **When did Sir Lancelot go on a date?**

A: At knight time.

Q: **How did the orange make time for his date?**

A: He squeezed it in.

Q: **How do you keep your girlfriend in suspense on Valentine's Day?**

A: I'll tell you later!

Q: **What's black, white, and red all over?**

A: A penguin that got a Valentine's Day kiss!

Knock, knock.

Who's there?

Sweet tea.

Sweet tea who?

Sweet tea, you're my valentine!

Q: Why did the boy go hunting with his date?

A: Because it only cost him a buck.

Q: Why did the boy want to date the professional skier?

A: She had a hill-arious sense of humor!

Knock, knock.

Who's there?

Pigeon.

Pigeon who?

Pigeon and help us get ready for the Valentine's party!

Q: Why do snowmen make bad boyfriends?

A: Because they're coldhearted!

Q: Why did the fish break up with the lobster?

A: Because he was shellfish.

Poodle: Are you sure you want to be my valentine?

Golden retriever: I'm paws-itive!

Q: Why did the girl eat her Valentine's candy before she went to bed?

A: She wanted sweet dreams.

Q: Why did the bike stay home on Valentine's Day?

A: It was two tired.

**Q: What is the best day to take your
date to the beach?**

A: Sun-day!

**Q: Why did the girl have a crush on a
skeleton?**

A: Because he was humerus.

**Q: What did the boulder say to his
girlfriend?**

A: "You rock!"

**Q: Why did the boy call the girl on
February 14th?**

A: Because she asked for a ring on Valentine's Day.

Knock, knock.

Who's there?

Alex.

Alex who?

Alex you one more time: Will you be my valentine?

Q: What did the rope do after it got engaged?

A: It tied the knot.

**Q: Why did the bumblebee keep star-
ing at his girlfriend?**

A: He thought she was bee-utiful!

**Q: What did the electric eel get for
Valentine's Day?**

A: A box of shock-let hearts!

**Q: Why did the skunks stay home on
Valentine's Day?**

A: They didn't have a scent to their
name!

Q: Why did the fireman propose to his girlfriend?

A: She set his heart on fire!

Q: Why did the snowflakes go on a date?

A: They were falling for each other.

Q: Why did the girl get carrots for Valentine's Day?

A: Some bunny loved her!

Q: What did the firefly say to his girl-friend?

A: "You light up my life!"

Q: **What do you get when you cross headphones and roses?**

A: Earbuds!

Q: **Why did the boa constrictor marry her boyfriend?**

A: He was her main squeeze.

Q: **Why did the snowman cancel his date for Valentine's Day?**

A: He was getting cold feet.

Q: **Why was the banker so sad on Valentine's Day?**

A: He felt loan-ly.

Q: Why did the bird get sick after its dinner date?

A: It had butterflies in its stomach.

Q: How did the mermaid feel when she dated a human?

A: Like a fish out of water.

Q: What did one light bulb say to the other?

A: "I love you a watt!"

Q: **Why did the carpenter give roses and chocolate for Valentine's Day?**

A: He knew the drill.

Q: **Where did the girl keep her love notes?**

A: In a valen-tin.

Sadie: Did you hear about the couple who fell in love on an airplane?

Susie: Yes, because love is in the air!

Q: What happened when the drum-mer fell in love?

A: His heart skipped a beat!

Q: What do you call two polar bears on a date in Hawaii?

A: Lost.

Knock, knock.

Who's there?

Gus.

Gus who?

Gus what I'm giving you for Valen-tine's Day!

Q: **What happened when the pigeons fell in love?**

A: They were lovey-dovey.

Knock, knock.

Who's there?

Jamaica.

Jamaica who?

Jamaica me happy!

Q: **What did the postal worker wear on Valentine's Day?**

A: Ad-dress.

I LOVE YOU

BE MINE

YOU ROCK

Q: Why did the snail cancel its Valentine's date?

A: It was feeling sluggish.

Knock, knock.

Who's there?

Whale.

Whale who?

Whale you be mine?

Knock, knock.

Who's there?

Pizza.

Pizza who?

You have a pizza my heart!

Q: Why was the girlfriend mad when she got a diamond for Valentine's Day?

A: Because it was a baseball diamond.

Knock, knock.

Who's there?

Handsome.

Handsome who?

Handsome valentines out to your friends today.

Q: Why did the chicken break up with the rooster?

A: He had a fowl mouth!

Q: What kind of Valentine's candy is never on time?

A: Choco-late.

Knock, knock.

Who's there?

Raymond.

Raymond who?

Raymond me to wish you a happy Valentine's Day!

Jackson: Would you like a date on Valentine's Day?

Jenny: I think I'd rather have some chocolate.

Q: **Why did the sock and shoe get married?**

A: They were sole mates.

Knock, knock.

Who's there?

Avenue.

Avenue who?

Avenue finished making your valentines yet?

Q: **What did the dairy farmer say to his wife?**

A: "You're my butter half!"

Q: Where did the spaghetti take its girlfriend on Valentine's Day?

A: To the meat-ball.

Q: What did the finger say to the nose on Valentine's Day?

A: "I'd pick you again!"

Knock, knock.

Who's there?

Mushroom.

Mushroom who?

I have mushroom in my heart for you.

Knock, knock.

Who's there?

Carmen.

Carmen who?

Carmen out on a date with me!

Q: Why did the moon go out with the sun?

A: It wanted to go on a hot date!

Knock, knock.

Who's there?

Alaska.

Alaska who?

Alaska to be my valentine.

Knock, knock.

Who's there?

Milton.

Milton who?

You're Milton my heart.

Knock, knock.

Who's there?

Liver.

Liver who?

I liver more every day.

Knock, knock.

Who's there?

Seymour.

Seymour who?

Do you Seymour friends who need a valentine?

Q: Why do snails like Valentine's Day?

A: They love to shell-ebrate!

Q: What did the horse do when she fell in love?

A: She got mare-ried.

Knock, knock.

Who's there?

Weasel.

Weasel who?

Weasel be late if you don't open the door!

Knock, knock.

Who's there?

Rhino.

Rhino who?

Rhino what we should do for Valentine's Day!

Q: Why should you fall in love with a baker?

A: They'll never dessert you!

Knock, knock.

Who's there?

Espresso.

Espresso who?

How do I espresso my love for you?

Knock, knock.

Who's there?

Kenya.

Kenya who?

Kenya pass out these valentines for me?

Q: Why did the cats have fun on Valentine's Day?

A: They were feline the love!

Q: How do light bulbs send love letters?

A: By lamp-post.

Q: What do you get from a slug on February 14th?

A: A valen-slime!

Q: How did the telephone propose to his girlfriend?

A: He gave her a ring.

Q: Why did the geologist break up with her boyfriend?

A: He took her for granite.

Q: What did the black widow spider say to her date?

A: "Will you be my dinner for Valentine's Day?"

Q: Why did the tornado go to the Valentine's dance?

A: It wanted to do the twist.

Q: What did Frankenstein say to his girlfriend?

A: "Will you be my Valenstein?"

Q: Why did the frog miss Valentine's Day?

A: He croaked before February 14th.

Knock, knock.

Who's there?

Arthur.

Arthur who?

Arthur any valentines for me?

- - - - - - - - - - - - - - - - - - - -

Knock, knock.

Who's there?

Wichita.

Wichita who?

Wichita chocolates are your favorite?

Q: What did the circle say to the triangle on Valentine's Day?

A: "I think you're acute!"

Q: How did Venus ask Saturn out for Valentine's Day?

A: She gave him a ring.

Q: What did the barista give his girl-friend for Valentine's Day?

A: Mugs and kisses.

Knock, knock.

Who's there?

Lafayette.

Lafayette who?

Did you Lafayette after all these jokes?

Knock, knock.

Who's there?

Quincy.

Quincy who?

I Quincy you're ready for Valentine's Day!

Q: Why did the pterodactyl have a bad time on Valentine Day?

A: Because her date was a dino-snore.

Q: What time did the dentist pick up his date?

A: Tooth-thirty.

Q: What kind of flowers make great friends?

A: Rosebuds.

Knock, knock.

Who's there?

Watson.

Watson who?

Watson the menu for Valentine's Day?

Q: Why didn't the skeleton ask the girl out on Valentine's Day?

A: He didn't have the guts.

Q: Why didn't the bear want any Valentine's candy?

A: It was already stuffed.

Q: What did the boy cat say to the girl cat?

A: "We're purr-fect for each other."

Q: Why was the nose still single?

A: It was too picky.

Knock, knock.

Who's there?

Duluth.

Duluth who?

Duluth tooth ith gonna keep me from eating my Valentine'th candy!

Q: What did the dog say on Valentine's Day?

A: "I woof you very much!"

Knock, knock.

Who's there?

Havana.

Havana who?

I'm Havana party for Valentine's Day.

    Want to come?

Knock, knock.

Who's there?

Oxford.

Oxford who?

I Oxford a valentine from all my

    friends.

Q: **What do you get when you cross two fish and a valentine?**

A: Guppy love.

Q: **What did the T. rex say to his girlfriend?**

A: "You're dino-mite!"

Jenny: **Did you hear that the cow and bull broke up?**

Holly: Yes, they won't stop beefing about it!

Q: **Why did the girl break up with the astronaut?**

A: He was a bit spacey.

Q: Why did the girl break up with the pastry chef?

A: He kept waffling.

Q: Where did the dolphins go on their Valentine's date?

A: A dive-in movie.

Q: What did the buck say to the doe?

A: "I'm fawned of you, deer."

Q: Why did the girl agree to go out with the dentist?

A: She didn't want to hurt his fillings.

- -

Knock, knock.

Who's there?

Whitney.

Whitney who?

**I can't Whitney longer to give you
your valentine.**

Knock, knock.

Who's there?

Honeybee.

Honeybee who?

**Honeybee a dear and give me a valen-
tine!**

Q: What do you call a bottle of free perfume?

A: Un-cent-ed!

Q: How do you know if a bird likes you?

A: It'll give you a tweet on Valentine's Day!

Q: Why did the boy have a crush on the baker?

A: She was a cutie-pie.

Knock, knock.

Who's there?

Italy.

Italy who?

Italy great when I get to open my valentines.

Q: What did the horse say to his girlfriend?

A: "Let's giddyup and go on a date!"

Q: How did the penguin make his valentines?

A: Igloo-ed them together.

Q: **What did the ribbon say to the rope on February 14th?**

A: "Will you be my valen-twine?"

Q: **What did Dracula say on Valentine's Day?**

A: "Let me count the ways I love you!"

Knock, knock.

Who's there?

Waffle.

Waffle who?

A waffle lot of valentines are in my mailbox!

Q: **Why did the boy take the girl out for coffee?**

A: He liked her a latte.

Knock, knock.

Who's there?

Lima bean.

Lima bean who?

Lima bean thinking you should be my valentine.

Q: **Did you hear about the couple who fell in love at the Indy 500?**

A: Their hearts were racing!

Q: Why did the scissors fall in love?

A: They made a fine pair!

Knock, knock.

Who's there?

Diesel.

Diesel who?

Diesel be the best Valentine's Day

ever!

Q: What did the shark say to the min-

now on Valentine's Day?

A: "I chews you!"

Knock, knock.

Who's there?

Alpine.

Alpine who?

Alpine away for you forever!

Q: What did the Labrador say to the chihuahua?

A: "You're so doggone cute!"

Knock, knock.

Who's there?

El Paso.

El Paso who?

El Paso valentine to all my friends.

Knock, knock

Who's there?

Philip.

Philip who?

Philip your valentine over to see who it's from.

Q: What do you get when you cross broccoli and roses?

A: Cauli-flowers!

Q: Why was the detective easy to surprise on Valentine's Day?

A: Because she was clue-less.

Lovebird #1: Should we make dinner reservations for Valentine's Day?

Lovebird #2: No, let's just wing it!

Q: What happened when all the cowboys rushed to mail their valentines?

A: There was a stamp-ede.

Pickle #1: I'm sorry I forgot your valentine!

Pickle #2: It's no big dill.

Bride: Should we go to Hawaii for our honeymoon?

Groom: I'd lava to!

Q: What did one woodworker say to the other?

A: "I have a whittle crush on you!"

Q: What did one sheep say to the other on Valentine's Day?

A: "I woolly love you!"

Knock, knock.

Who's there?

Pudding.

Pudding who?

I'm pudding the final touches on my valentines.

Knock, knock.

Who's there?

Lena.

Lena who?

Lena little closer and I'll whisper, "I love you!"

Q: **Why did the caterpillar break up with the grasshopper?**

A: They kept bugging each other.

Knock, knock.

Who's there?

Justin.

Justin who?

Justin time to deliver my valentines!

Knock, knock.

Who's there?

Wanda.

Wanda who?

Wanda be my valentine?

Q: What did one wolf say to the other?

A: "Howl always be your valentine!"

Q: What did one caramel say to the other?

A: "Let's stick together."

Q: What did the tiger say to the elephant?

A: "Zoo want to be my valentine?"

Q: **What did the sea lion say to the beaver?**

A: "Will you be my significant otter?"

Knock, knock.

Who's there?

Dora.

Dora who?

You're a-dora-ble!

Q: **Why don't dalmatians take a bath before their date?**

A: They don't want to be spotless.

Knock, knock.

Who's there?

Sofa.

Sofa who?

Sofa I've received a lot of valentines.

Knock, knock.

Who's there?

Mint.

Mint who?

We're mint to be together!

Knock, knock.

Who's there?

Koala.

Koala who?

Open the door so we can have some koala-ty time!

Knock, knock.

Who's there?

Soda.

Soda who?

I soda have a crush on you!

Q: What did the duck say to his girl-friend?

A: "Waddle I do without you?"

Q: Why did the candles go out for Valentine's Day?

A: They were a match made in heaven!

Q: Why did the koalas get married?

A: Because life apart would be un-bearable.

Q: Why did the bull go broke after Valentine's Day?

A: He spent too much mooo-la on his date.

Q: What did the glue say to the paper?

A: "I'm stuck on you!"

- -

Q: What did the twig say to the log?

A: "I'll stick with you."

Q: Did you hear about the dogs who got married?

A: They had a fairy-tail wedding!

Knock, knock.

Who's there?

Owen.

Owen who?

I'm Owen you another valentine.

Q: What needs a big hug on Valentine's Day?

A: A blue whale!

Knock, knock.

Who's there?

Waiter.

Waiter who?

Waiter you doing for Valentine's Day?

Knock, knock.

Who's there?

Albert.

Albert who?

Albert you get a lot of valentines this year!

Q: What did the frog wear to the Valentine's dance?

A: Open-toad shoes.

Q: Why is it fun to date a farmer?

A: They're full of beans!

Q: Why did the girl break up with the butcher?

A: He was full of baloney!

Knock, knock.

Who's there?

Woodrow.

Woodrow who?

Woodrow like to go out with me on Valentine's Day?

Knock, knock.

Who's there?

Sierra.

Sierra who?

Sierra later at the Valentine's party!

Q: What did the mittens say on Valentine's Day?

A: "I glove you!"

Knock, knock.

Who's there?

Thumb.

Thumb who?

Thumb-body loves you!

Knock, knock.

Who's there?

Sapphire.

Sapphire who?

Sapphire this is the best Valentine's Day ever!

Q: Did you hear about the runner whose date stood him up?

A: His hopes were dashed!

Knock, knock.

Who's there?

Stella.

Stella who?

You Stella piece of my heart!

Q: Why did the golden retriever have a crush on the poodle?

A: He thought she looked fetching.

Q: Did you hear about the soccer players who broke up?

A: They were good sports about it.

Q: What do you call it when farmers get married?

A: Grow-mantic!

Q: Why did the squash break up with the corn?

A: It was ear-ritating!

Q: Why did the girl have a crush on the sailor?

A: He was easy on the aye-ayes.

Tree #1: Will you go on a date with me?

Tree #2: Oaky-doke!

Q: How much does it cost to give a skunk a valentine?

A: Fifty scents!

Q: What did the butterfly say to the ladybug?

A: "You make my heart flutter."

Knock, knock.

Who's there?

Distress.

Distress who?

Distress is the perfect thing to wear for Valentine's Day.

- -

Q: What did the dogs have to eat on their date?

A: Macaroni and fleas.

Q: Why should you date a teacher when you grow up?

A: They have a lot of class.

Girl: Should we go sailing or canoeing on our date?

Boy: It's either-oar.

Q: Why is the shark still single?

A: It's too fin-icky!

Q: Why did the girl break up with the archer?

A: He was too arrow-gant.

Q: How do you get a cat to go out with you?

A: Be purr-sistent.

Q: Why did the broccoli break up with the cabbage?

A: It had a big head.

Q: Why couldn't the race car driver pick out a valentine?

A: He was Indy-cisive!

Q: Why were the shoes still single?

A: They were de-feet-ed in love.

Q: What did the bulldozer say to the dump truck?

A: "I dig you!"

Q: **What did the bagel say to the bread?**

A: "I like the way you roll!"

Q: **Why shouldn't you take your date to the gym?**

A: It might not work out.

Q: **How do skunks know if they're right for each other?**

A: They trust their in-stinks.

Q: **Why did the pirate finally tell his girlfriend he loved her?**

A: He had to get it off his chest.

Q: **How does a chicken send a valentine?**

A: In a hen-velope!

Q: **Why did the monster get married?**

A: He was the man of her screams.

Q: **Where does a squirrel find a date for Valentine's Day?**

A: On the inter-nut!

Q: **What do you get when you cross a piano and a valentine?**

A: A love note!

Q: What do you get when you cross a bee and a cupcake?

A: Fro-sting!

Q: Why did the gardener give her boyfriend a valentine?

A: It was a budding romance.

Knock, knock.

Who's there?

Wheelbarrow.

Wheelbarrow who?

I wheelbarrow a stamp to mail my val-

entine.

Q: Did you hear about the pilots who

fell in love?

A: It was love at first flight.

Q: **What does a dog wear on Valentine's Day?**

A: Pants!

Q: **What did the lemon say to the orange?**

A: "You're my main squeeze!"

Q: **Why did the girl break up with the swimmer?**

A: He went off the deep end.

Q: **What did the pole vaulter say to her boyfriend?**

A: "I'll never get over you!"

Q: **What did the pepperoni say to the mushroom?**

A: "You stole a pizza my heart!"